Anger Management

An Introduction To Anger Management For Parents: Recognizing And Coping With Its Effects On Your Family And Your Children

(A No-nonsense Approach To Managing Your Anger And Staying Out Of Difficult Circumstances)

Achill Manolas

TABLE OF CONTENT

What Is Anger? 1

Engage In The Cultivation Of Mindfulness, Meditation, And Forgiveness As Part Of A Regular Routine. 7

Understanding The Factors Influencing Personal Motivation 51

Alternative Approaches For The Management Of Anger, Anxiety, And Stress 61

Addressing The Physiological Effects Of Anger 71

The Regulation Of Emotional Responses 80

Developing An Understanding Of The Individuals With Whom One Interacts Is Crucial. 88

Acknowledging The Presence Of An Anger-Related Condition 103

The Sociocultural Factors Contributing To The Experience Of Anger. 130

Assuming Accountability For One's Anger 148

What Is Anger?

Anger is an affective state that serves as an indicator of a perceived discrepancy or violation. This may indicate that an external entity or circumstance has impeded the achievement of one's objectives, caused disillusionment, or subjected one to mistreatment. The experience of anger can elicit a range of responses, including the inclination to engage in self-defense, aggression, or seeking retribution.

Anger is a universally experienced emotion that can manifest in different intensities among individuals. However, the detrimental impact of anger arises when its magnitude or recurrence hinders one's mental well-being, legal status, occupational productivity, or interpersonal connections.

According to popular belief, anger is considered to be the most potent emotional state. Due of this particular factor, it is prone to being misinterpreted. Anger can be triggered by three primary factors: frustration, perceived threat, and criticism. Individuals may experience a sense of moderate anger in response to the actions of specific individuals or when circumstances deviate from their intended course. Anger may also be experienced in conjunction with feelings of sadness.

The subjective experiences of an individual, including their sensations, emotions, and mood, are discrete entities that exhibit interconnectedness. The affective reaction of an individual has the potential to influence their subjective perception and evaluation of various phenomena. The emotion of anger is not solely confined to the realm of cognition, but is also outwardly manifested through nonverbal cues and bodily expressions. Individuals may have physiological responses such as an elevated heart rate or perspiration on their hands in the presence of anger.

The identification of anger in individuals can frequently be ascertained from their verbal communication patterns and facial cues. The act of fixating one's gaze, tightly gripping one's hands, and displaying a downward curvature of the lips are among several commonly observed nonverbal cues that indicate the presence of anger in an individual. Nevertheless, certain individuals possess the ability to internalize their anger rather than overtly manifesting it, thereby rendering its detection less apparent.

When uncontrolled, rage can have detrimental consequences. The aforementioned issue can give rise to challenges in both one's personal and professional spheres, as well as their social interactions. The individual may experience a heightened emotional state that appears to have the potential to erupt uncontrollably. The regulation of rage intensity may be beyond an individual's control, although the manner in which it is manifested can be subject to personal management.

The emotion of anger should not be categorized as inherently negative or undesirable.

There exists a widespread misperception among individuals that rage is a predominantly unpleasant emotional state. Anger, while occasionally powerful, is not inherently a negative emotion. Anger can also be perceived as a constructive emotional experience. The experience of perceiving injustice might serve as a catalyst for individuals to assert their rights and advocate for themselves.

Through the process of channeling his fury, Martin Luther King, Jr. effectively disseminated his ideology of nonviolence, thereby emerging as a source of inspiration for a multitude of others. Anger and violent behavior should be distinguished as separate phenomena. Unrestrained anger has the potential to manifest as hostility or, in extreme cases, escalate into acts of violence. Nevertheless, the emotion of rage can be effectively managed to prevent its escalation into acts of violence.

Numerous studies have demonstrated the interconnectedness of our diverse range of emotions. It has been established that fear serves as the fundamental emotion from which all other emotions originate. Several emotions that might be triggered by fear include jealousy, disgust, and fury. When an individual experiences dread towards a particular entity or situation, it is not uncommon for them to eventually develop feelings of anger directed towards themselves due to their perceived lack of courage in their response.

Fear and rage are two emotions that exhibit significant similarities. Both stimuli elicit a same physiological reaction from our autonomic nerve system. Anger and fear share a commonality in that emotions encompass elements of conflict, regret, control, and purpose. Control has a substantial influence on each of these emotional states. When individuals experience fear, they undergo a sensation of diminished control, leading to the emergence of uncertainty and a sense of unease.

Engage In The Cultivation Of Mindfulness, Meditation, And Forgiveness As Part Of A Regular Routine.

The presence of anger, whether expressed passively or openly, has the potential to cause significant disruption in one's life. As one enhances their ability to identify sources of anger, it becomes imperative to cultivate the skill of relinquishing agitation, irritation, and aggravation, and instead fostering a state of tranquility and contentment. The subsequent tactics facilitate the accomplishment of said objective.

The concept of "forgive and forget" refers to the act of pardoning someone for a wrongdoing and thereafter erasing the memory of the transgression.

The act of forgiveness serves as a comforting remedy for vulnerable emotional injuries, a principle that applies to both self-forgiveness and forgiveness of others. Persisting in harboring resentment against another individual will ultimately result in self-inflicted emotional distress.

The experience of ruminating on past grievances can intensify one's emotional distress. Likewise, should one persistently dwell upon past errors and disappointments that have caused personal distress, it is probable that self-criticism and emotional distress would intensify. The feeling of dissatisfaction gradually transforms into a state of fury. In order to enhance one's personal growth, it is advisable to engage in the practice of self-forgiveness and extend forgiveness towards others. Disregard negative events, extract valuable lessons from them, and progress forward.

It is recommended to allocate a designated time slot of 10 to 20 minutes every week for introspection, whereby one can contemplate about personal aspects encompassing past failures, blunders, and adverse life experiences that have caused emotional distress up until the present day. Reflecting upon personal experiences and engaging in introspection can be valuable for those seeking personal growth and emotional well-being. One approach to this process is documenting one's thoughts using audio recordings or engaging in deep contemplation. By selectively revisiting and analyzing negative memories that evoke feelings of self-discontent and rage, individuals can potentially gain insights into their emotional triggers and work towards personal improvement. One potential example is to an individual's involvement in a motor vehicle collision some years ago, which was attributed to their impaired state due to alcohol consumption. Another instance involves the consistent accumulation of financial deficits within one's entrepreneurial endeavors. Regardless of the underlying motivation, it is imperative to engage in thoughtful contemplation and construct a vivid mental representation of the subject matter at hand.

Visualize the gradual expansion of the mental representation as one experiences heightened self-directed fury, and upon perceiving the culmination of this emotional state, envision the utilization of a sharp, pointed needle to puncture and then deflate the enlarged mental construct. Imagine the release of all your wrath as it dissipates from your physical being. Engage in deep inhalations and exhale more extensively in the process. Simultaneously, engage in the repetitive recitation of the phrase, "I extend forgiveness to myself and am prepared to progress forward," either internally or audibly. Engaging in this practice on a weekly basis will likely result in an increased sense of tranquility.

It is advisable to refrain from frequent contemplation of personal or interpersonal distressing experiences, with the intention of minimizing the recollection of one's own or others' past events. Whenever one's mind becomes distracted and recalls a negative experience that elicits feelings of anger, it is advisable to cultivate mindfulness by actively engaging in the current work at hand. When preparing a dinner, it is important to carefully consider the selection of components that are added to the wok. When engaging in the act of movie-watching, it is imperative to diligently direct one's attention towards the unfolding events within the picture. Each instance in which an individual recollects a distressing encounter, it is recommended to physically gesture by shaking one's head and audibly uttering the phrase, "I am directing my attention towards the current moment."

It is imperative to extend forgiveness to individuals who have purposefully or accidentally caused harm, while also seeking reconciliation with the negative encounter as a whole. It is vital to comprehend two significant factors. Initially, it is imperative to acknowledge that although the actions of the individual in question may have caused emotional distress and dissatisfaction, it is plausible that they possessed a rational justification for their behavior. Individuals possess the inherent entitlement to engage in actions that align with their personal convictions, a domain over which external influence is limited.

Furthermore, it is imperative to acknowledge the reality that events that have transpired are immutable and cannot be altered retroactively, regardless of one's fervent desire to do so. Instead of harboring resentments and simmering with indignation, it is advisable to practice forgiveness and progress forward. There are two alternative approaches to addressing this matter: one can engage in internal forgiveness, whereby the individual forgives the person in their thoughts, or one can opt for direct confrontation with the individual involved, expressing their readiness to progress and potentially even engaging in a physical embrace. Nevertheless, in the event that this someone is no longer an active participant in one's life, it is advisable to release oneself from the emotional distress associated with that particular grievance.

Engage in the aforementioned practice of self-forgiveness for a minimum of five minutes each day, as doing so is expected to result in a reduction of negative emotions associated with the particular event and individual.

When it comes to granting forgiveness in a face-to-face context, it is advisable to initiate contact with the individual in question, arrange a meeting, and engage in a conversation regarding the specific incident or experience. In the event that errors have been made, it is advisable to acknowledge and accept them. However, it is important to refrain from exerting pressure on others to do so. Expressing a willingness to adapt and indicating a desire for the individual to be included in one's life, it is conveyed that one is prepared to embrace their presence. It is advisable to express the latter sentiment solely if one genuinely desires to maintain communication with the individual in question.

Incorporate forgiveness as a regular practice in your daily life, enabling a gradual process of self-forgiveness and forgiveness towards others immediately upon experiencing emotional distress. Simultaneously, it is imperative to ascertain and recognize the principal insights and teachings derived from an unfavorable encounter, in order to avoid repeating similar errors. Engaging in self-improvement endeavors can be an effective strategy for mitigating rage.

Progressive muscle relaxation (PMR) is a therapeutic technique that involves systematically tensing and then relaxing different muscle groups in the body. This method aims to reduce muscle tension

The relaxation exercise entails a two-step procedure wherein one actively engages in the deliberate tensing and subsequent relaxing of different muscle groups inside the body. By engaging in this practice, the body is deceived into perceiving a state of non-engagement in a flight or fight situation, as a result of the profound relaxation experienced by all the muscles. Consequently, the assumption is made that no adverse events occur when the body is in a relaxed state. In addition, this practice will facilitate a heightened level of familiarity with the sensation of tension that typically precedes an expression of anger, specifically in relation to distinct bodily regions. Consequently, this will facilitate the individual's ability to maintain a state of heightened awareness towards their triggers, enabling them to implement appropriate measures as necessary. Ultimately, the integration of deep breathing techniques can be employed in conjunction with this exercise to optimize outcomes.

Prior to commencing this exercise, it is imperative to seek medical advice from a healthcare professional if you have a pre-existing medical condition such as back difficulties, muscular spasms, or other related injuries that may potentially be exacerbated by engaging in this activity. In the initial phase, it is advisable to locate a position of comfort for sitting. It is recommended to ensure that one's attire is sufficiently loose and that footwear is not worn.

Once prepared, it is advisable to engage in a series of deep, soothing inhalations and exhalations in order to achieve a state of mental clarity. Subsequently, it is recommended to direct one's complete concentration towards the right foot. Direct your attention towards the musculature of your foot and exert maximum force by contracting them forcefully. Once the maximum level of compression has been achieved, it is recommended to maintain that position for a duration of 10 seconds. Subsequently, it is advisable to fully rest your foot for an additional duration of 10 seconds, while contemplating the disparity between the two aforementioned conditions.

The subsequent step involves replicating the aforementioned procedure with the left foot, followed by a continuation in a similar manner until the entire body has been addressed. Initially, individuals may encounter difficulties in selectively contracting the specific muscles they intend to engage. However, through consistent practice, one should eventually attain proficiency in effectively isolating the desired target regions. Ideally, it is recommended to engage in a comprehensive circuit training routine that encompasses all major muscle groups of the body, including the feet, calves, thighs, buttocks, stomach, chest, back, arms, hands, shoulders, neck, and face, throughout each workout session.

The sense of frustration is a common phenomenon that does not require explicit elucidation. It is highly likely that individuals have encountered a multitude of irritating circumstances. Minor inconveniences, although capable of generating significant levels of aggravation. The mosquito that was previously mentioned? When the object is repeatedly positioned over one's facial region for the one hundredth occurrence, it signifies the commencement of a conflict.

Common sources of irritation encompass several aspects such as the persistent malfunctioning of writing instruments, the presence of a colleague engaging in the disruptive activity of tether-ball, the ceaseless influx of unsolicited guidance from one's maternal figure, the superordinate who consistently disregards one's input, and the perception of expended exertion yielding little outcomes.

The third stage: Fury.

The manner in which it becomes evident: It might be asserted that the situation has become significantly more serious. The emotion of fury holds greater significance due to its cumulative effect on an individual's emotional state. You have surpassed the boiling point and have exhibited a state of emotional eruption, my acquaintance. Feelings of annoyance and frustration have escalated into an intense state of uncontrolled anger, providing a sense of relief in being able to express it. The trigger serves as a means of salvation.

The individual in question appears to have lost faith in their ability to engage in logical reasoning, since they have deviated from a coherent line of thinking. You are experiencing a state of anger and you desire to express this emotion to a global audience. Furthermore, even in the absence of explicit communication, observers possess the ability to discern one's emotional state by the manifestation of physical behaviors such as kicking and shouting. Fury exhibits vocalization, violence, and serves as a cathartic outlet. The film "Fury" possesses a cinematic quality due to its authentic portrayal of the unbridled expression of human passion. The phenomenon under consideration possesses certain health benefits, albeit with the potential to rapidly and readily transition into hazardous terrain.

What elicits feelings of intense anger within you: What fails to elicit feelings of intense anger within you? After an extended duration of enduring unfavorable circumstances, you have reached your breaking point. The trigger can encompass a wide range of stimuli, including an inopportune utterance of an inappropriate term, a sudden computer malfunction, or even a seemingly insignificant error that would typically go unnoticed. When one's rage possesses such immense power, all things become permissible.

Numerous sources of frustration are commonly encountered, such as the absence of logical reasoning, offensive remarks, disregard for others, political figures, extended family members, one's marital partner, instances of unfairness, and so forth.

Childhood is a developmental stage characterized by frequent episodes of anger and irrational behavior exhibited by children. Consider a scenario wherein an adult exhibits a display of emotional distress within a retail establishment subsequent to their spouse's denial of a purchase request. Instances of adults displaying temper tantrums are not uncommon, however such behavior is generally regarded as socially unacceptable and widely recognized as wrong.

The acquisition of anger management skills is often initiated throughout childhood by a significant number of individuals. Individuals are sometimes advised against adopting an excessively serious demeanor or approaching problems with undue impatience. The acquisition of the ability to express remorse for causing harm to others and the practice of being advised to engage in calming activities as a means of achieving emotional well-being are integral aspects of our social development. Nevertheless, the comprehensive understanding of anger and the ongoing management of its enduring emotional effects are not usually well addressed in our education. Certain experiences encountered throughout childhood may contribute to the development of unresolved anger, which may subsequently manifest in maladaptive expressions during maturity. For instance, a young male child may have been regularly instructed to exhibit stoicism and suppress emotions by conforming to societal expectations of masculinity, resulting in a distorted perception of gender roles. According to Dittmann (2003), individuals who are consistently instructed to suppress their emotions during childhood may develop violent tendencies, exhibiting a propensity for reactive aggression as a means of safeguarding their perceived masculinity.

When individuals grapple with shame, it has the potential to elicit emotions characterized by a profound dislike or hatred towards oneself. This phenomenon might lead to self-reflection and introspection. Indeed, empirical research has indicated that approximately 50% of incarcerated women have acknowledged experiencing ideations of self-inflicted injury as a consequence of the profound guilt stemming from childhood abuse.

Although individual differences exist, previous studies have indicated that both men and women generally experience comparable levels of rage.

However, women tend to internalize their anger, whilst males tend to externalize it. When individuals experience anger, they often have a desire to externalize or express their emotions. This could involve engaging in verbal confrontations with someone in close proximity and deliberately exacerbating their distress to match one's own. Alternatively, individuals may choose to internalize their emotions and manifest them through self-destructive behaviors, such as engaging in various forms of self-harm.

The experience of enduring persistent physical and psychological abuse from one's parents, coupled with an inability to effectively express anger, has the potential to contribute to the development of anger-related difficulties in adulthood. The inability to express our feelings hinders our comprehensive understanding of their significance. Without a comprehensive understanding of the characteristics and attributes associated with being an individual who experiences emotions deeply, it becomes challenging to identify and adopt constructive methods of articulating and manifesting these sentiments in a manner that promotes overall well-being. This phenomenon has the potential to result in the repression of our emotional experiences, subsequently giving rise to episodes of furious outbursts and intense, hot encounters.

There exist certain inquiries one must pose to oneself in order to ascertain whether one's childhood surpasses that of others. Firstly, how did you observe your parents' responses to anger? Did they frequently experience distress? Did they engage in abusive behavior? Were you subjected to feelings of shame due to circumstances beyond your control? The manner in which individuals' parents have managed their emotions can serve as a reliable indicator of their own approach to emotional regulation.

The passivity exhibited by your mother does not necessarily imply that you possess the same trait. Both individuals may exhibit emotional repression, but through distinct mechanisms.

According to Sigmund Freud, anger serves as a social signal to communicate potential threats in a manner that aligns with evolutionary principles. When individuals perceive a discrepancy or problem, they tend to respond with great enthusiasm in order to communicate their desire for assistance in resolving the situation. The potential impact of anger on inducing fear in others and the role of irritation as a signal for addressing underlying emotional concerns are often not fully recognized by individuals (Potegal, 2010).

In certain instances, the acquisition of anger as a means of self-expression may have been facilitated through instruction or guidance. Upon returning home from work and experiencing a distressing day, individuals may resort to actions such as forcefully closing cupboards and stomping their feet as a means of communicating their negative emotional state to their cohabitants. Likewise, individuals may inquire, "What is the matter?" upon perceiving audible expressions of discomfort. The subconscious mind may endeavor to seek assistance, and one can effectively address this anger by simply inquiring about the possibility of engaging in a conversation with another individual and articulating one's emotions in a constructive and beneficial manner.

The experience of unhappiness has the potential to induce feelings of tension and anxiety, which in turn might give rise to the manifestation of rage. Persistent dissatisfaction with one's occupation, interpersonal conflicts, and a negative self-perception can contribute to prolonged periods of misery. The human brain may endeavor to rectify situations that deviate from the expected norms of existence. Anger may serve as a potential mechanism for resolving conflicts, since it can be employed to exert control over the situation.

The disparities experienced during our childhood may contribute to the accumulation of anger inside our societal framework. Living in poverty or experiencing other forms of socioeconomic disparity might potentially lead to feelings of resentment towards individuals who possess greater wealth or resources. Rather than acknowledging the diverse range of challenges individuals face, there is a tendency to narrow our attention exclusively to our own difficulties, erroneously attributing our own tragedy to the happiness of others.

Passive aggression refers to a behavioral pattern characterized by indirect expressions of hostility, resentment, or anger.

The majority of individuals exhibit a reluctance to face the one responsible for their frustration. Furthermore, this phenomenon is also seen in those who adopt this particular manner of expressing rage. Nevertheless, they are not individuals who will succumb without putting up a fight. This behavior is attributable to individuals expressing their displeasure by actions that are intentionally contrary to the preferences of others, while asserting that such actions are either fortuitous or unintentional.

This particular manifestation of rage is considered highly detrimental, mostly because it fails to address the underlying cause of the issue. This exacerbates the situation, as the recipient likewise experiences frustration and may respond in a retaliatory manner. Ultimately, individuals do not attain a state of happiness.

Sarcasm is a form of communication that involves the use of irony, often with a

The majority of individuals have been socialized to refrain from openly expressing negative feelings, as doing so may have detrimental effects on their reputation. Nevertheless, individuals are compelled to articulate their dissatisfaction through various means. One potential approach to achieve this objective is to convey the message indirectly by presenting it in the form of a joke. It is like to achieving two objectives simultaneously. Ultimately, it might be argued that the aforementioned statement is merely a humorous remark.

Despite the use of subtle means to convey dissatisfaction, the sentiment is nevertheless seen and received in a humorous manner. Consequently, if the interlocutor fails to approach the matter with due gravity and regards it merely as a source of entertainment, one may find oneself increasingly exasperated. Alternatively, the scenario may unfold in a manner that the one being addressed perceives the matter with earnestness, interpreting one's actions as mockery, so resulting in a potential conflict. However, akin to the aforementioned rage styles, this approach will not effectively end the disagreement.

Understanding the underlying reasons for variations in individuals' susceptibility to anger can facilitate comprehension of such individuals. Moreover, it is possible to assist both oneself and others by providing information on anger management, an intervention strategy aimed at enhancing emotional regulation and self-control.

3. Determine the origins of one's anger issue.

It has been argued that the primary concern is often not the apparent problem at hand. In the context of religious texts, rage is metaphorically shown as a fruit, implying its origin from a tree. The underlying causes of most rage issues can be traced back to deeper psychological or emotional factors. Request divine intervention to assist in discerning the underlying factors contributing to one's experience of anger, so enabling the individual to effectively confront and resolve the matter at its fundamental source. Additionally, it is important to take into account these prevalent factors that contribute to the experience of anger:

The experience of pain or maltreatment in previous generations can result in the establishment of enduring patterns of behavior and thought, commonly referred to as generational strongholds.

Incorrect modeling

The experience of goal frustration

The term "offence" refers to an act or behavior that violates established rules, norms

One common phenomenon experienced by individuals is the occurrence of unmet expectations from others.

The concept of pride and loss are two significant themes that have been explored in various academic disciplines.

Misconceptions Regarding the Divine Methods (Unresolved Supplications)

The topic of discussion is to the psychological phenomenon known as insecurity, specifically referring to the inferiority complex.

The process of identifying the sources of one's anger can facilitate a more expeditious attainment of deliverance.

It is advisable to engage in patient and devoted prayer, seeking the guidance and intervention of the LORD.

When engaging in prayer, individuals create space for the Holy Spirit to eradicate the seeds of malevolence residing within the depths of their being. We give the opportunity for divine intervention to facilitate our healing and liberation from any form of psychological or spiritual constraint that restricts our freedom.

I highly encourage engaging in prayer and fasting as a means to address and seek resolution for any issues related to anger management. According to the biblical account in Matthew 17:21, Jesus asserted that certain spiritual matters necessitate the employment of prayer and fasting as the exclusive means of resolution. Anger issues are considered to be one of those instances.

When individuals engage in fasting and prayer as a means to attain liberation from a habit or stronghold, they create an opportunity for divine illumination to penetrate the depths of their being. According to Isaiah 58:6,

Is it not the fast that I chose, to dismantle the connections of immorality, to dismantle the bindings of oppression, to release the oppressed and shatter every form of enslavement? The user's text does not contain any information to rewrite.

Engaging in fasting and prayer with the intention of seeking release and liberation from the influence of Satan, both for ourselves and others, aligns with the divine purpose. When individuals align their actions with the divine will, they are bestowed with favors and achieve triumph.

This book provides a comprehensive set of prayer points and instructions aimed at effectively addressing and managing anger. By engaging in these prayers, one can attain deliverance from anger difficulties and other psychological barriers that impede personal growth.

Day 13: Engage in a Romantic Outing

Do you currently have a spouse or are you involved in a romantic partnership? Devote a day to spending quality time with your romantic spouse. Engage in a social outing. Attend a film screening. Please enjoy a cup of coffee. An excursion within a green space. Alternatively, engage in a romantic activity. The establishment of a mutually beneficial and supportive connection has the potential to foster a state of mental well-being. A sound mental state is conducive to experiencing authentic enjoyment. The experience of happiness serves as a countermeasure against unpleasant emotions and superfluous cognitive processes. Therefore, it is advisable to get outside and allocate the remaining portion of the day in the company of individuals who hold a significant place in your affections. In addition to fostering personal happiness, engaging in this behavior also contributes to the development of a robust interpersonal bond with one's spouse.

It is advisable to enhance one's listening skills. The act of listening encompasses more than simply perceiving auditory stimuli. It entails ensuring that individuals perceive themselves as being acknowledged and listened to. Engaging in active listening enhances one's capacity for empathy and facilitates a comprehensive understanding of the broader context from the perspectives of all parties involved.

Demonstrate benevolence towards others through the abstention from engaging in criticism, judgment, or condemnation. In contrast, the demonstration of kindness is manifested via the act of exhibiting respect and reverence for someone. Engage in the pursuit of combating negative elements and engaging in positive actions. By engaging in this behavior, individuals are instructing themselves that anger is not the sole or optimal approach for managing certain situations. However, via the demonstration of respect and reverence for individuals, one can foster an environment conducive to the establishment of peace.

Consider the manner in which one engages in conversation with acquaintances and individuals held dear. Do you communicate with them in a harsh manner? Do you consistently employ sarcasm? Do you engage in the act of labeling individuals using derogatory terms? In the context of close interpersonal relationships, individuals may experience a heightened sense of comfort that might lead to engaging in activities that are perceived as enjoyable, although may not align with objective assessments of amusement or satisfaction. Demonstrate acts of benevolence towards your acquaintances by exhibiting reverence and esteem towards them. In order to engage in a constructive and respectful conversation, it is advisable to refrain from engaging in derogatory language or name-calling. Instead, it is recommended to adopt a cool and composed demeanor while communicating with others. Furthermore, focusing on expressing positive sentiments can contribute to fostering a more harmonious and productive dialogue.

In a state of heightened anger, individuals frequently neglect to contemplate the potential consequences of their verbal expressions towards others. It is common for individuals to express unpleasant remarks. Human beings often fail to consider the emotions and perspectives of others, instead prioritizing their own immediate concerns. Today, engage in a brief soliloquy and envision yourself immersed in a highly charged scenario involving an individual with whom you share a deep emotional bond. One should engage in self-inquiry and critically evaluate the most appropriate course of action in a given situation.

The recommended course of action is as follows: Consider the following inquiries: In the event that I am upset by someone, should I retaliate by engaging in verbal aggression and uttering harsh remarks? Is engaging in derogatory remarks towards an individual the most effective approach to address the given circumstances?

Does the act of using harmful language contribute to personal growth and development?

Was the alleged perpetrator's intention truly to cause offense towards me? Alternatively, could it be possible that I am misinterpreting the signals or exaggerating their significance?

Upon introspection of these inquiries, it is advisable to contemplate a constructive approach to address them, and then employ the obtained insights throughout future instances of relational strain with an individual held dear.

The Influence of Anger

In certain circumstances, a moderate level of anger might prove beneficial and necessary, such as when confronting an exploitative employer or responding assertively to an abusive individual. However, in the majority of situations, anger tends to exert a predominantly adverse influence on our well-being.

Typically, the prevailing response to anger, regardless of its intensity ranging from slight annoyance to physical tension, manifests in the form of verbal aggression, which, once uttered, becomes irrevocable. In moments of rage, individuals often neglect to consider the potential impact of their actions on the individuals they criticize. These individuals may encompass various relationships, including loved ones such as friends, spouses, parents, children, as well as individuals with whom they have limited familiarity or are complete strangers. It is a common tendency for individuals to express highly impolite and injurious language when experiencing anger, and such verbal expressions frequently serve as a catalyst for the deterioration of relationships, friendships, and professional trajectories.

It is crucial to consider the physiological alterations that occur within our bodies during episodes of intense rage. These alterations have the potential to induce cardiovascular events, hypertension, and various other perilous health issues.

Certain individuals exhibit destructive and violent behavior when experiencing anger, resulting in the deliberate destruction of their personal belongings and important assets during episodes of intense emotional distress. This phenomenon may also encompass instances where individuals sustain physical harm as a consequence.

The experience of anger can lead individuals to make erroneous decisions that have the potential to cause harm to both themselves and others. Expressions such as vocally proclaiming "I resign!" or "I am terminating our marital union!" or simply uttering sentiments like "I deeply regret your return!" possess the potential to instigate alterations in one's life that may be undesirable.

Indeed, the ability to regulate and oversee one's emotions, particularly anger, holds significant importance. This book serves as a comprehensive guide for effectively managing anger-related challenges.

Principle #6: Establish communication with individuals

Certain issues may exceed an individual's capacity to manage independently. In instances where one experiences a combination of anger and helplessness, it is important to overcome any feelings of shame and seek support from a trusted someone with whom one may engage in conversation. These individuals has the potential to provide assistance, however the extent of their aid may vary. However, their mere act of attentively listening to your difficulties can be of great assistance. Potential individuals who could fulfill the role of a significant other in one's life include siblings, friends, romantic partners, or parents. It is advisable to promptly communicate with or arrange a meeting with an individual in order to express grievances or frustrations when experiencing anger.

If an individual continues to experience a sense of being overwhelmed by their anger, it is worth noting that some localities provide the services of experienced psychiatrists and therapists who possess the expertise to assist in addressing such concerns. Professionals in the field possess the ability to assist individuals in recognizing and managing their difficulties, as well as guiding them throughout the journey of rehabilitation.

Rule number seven entails the task of identifying and determining the appropriate resolution or remedy.

Undoubtedly, the individual have the exclusive capacity to identify and address the underlying issues that give rise to their experience of anger. The responsibility for managing one's anger ultimately lies with the individual, potentially with the assistance of others, as it is a personal attribute that cannot be regulated by other parties.

This point is germane to the initial point, wherein one must ascertain the underlying cause that is precipitating one's wrath. Now is the opportune moment to revisit the inquiry: what is the underlying cause of your anger?

Subsequently, proceed to seek a resolution.

Is your current emotional state characterized by anger due to the stress experienced in your professional occupation? Do you possess a negative disposition towards your occupation? It may be prudent to consider seeking alternative employment opportunities. Do you experience tension due to the perpetual disarray of your living space and the lack of available time to address the issue through cleaning? It may be advisable to consider using a professional domestic cleaner to assist with your household tasks. Are you a caregiver who remains at home and experiences fatigue while seeing to three children independently? Engage the services of an au-pair and contemplate reentering the workforce.

It is imperative to identify and address the underlying causes of one's anger and irritation in order to attain a state of enhanced tranquility, improved well-being, and heightened relaxation.

Understanding The Factors Influencing Personal Motivation

The regulation of anger holds significant importance, especially for individuals who exhibit a propensity for quick and intense emotional reactions. It is equally vital to comprehend, yet, that each individual have their own threshold. The initial phase in surmounting these constraints involves comprehending them.

Numerous elements will influence an individual's level of patience. Indeed, the degree of one's patience is subject to variation across different circumstances. Although individual differences may influence this particular characteristic, there exist some elements that can be examined. The aforementioned items encompass:

The topic of discussion pertains to one's individual personality traits. The influence of genetics on this matter is significant, leaving limited room for intervention. Individuals vary in their levels of impulsivity and susceptibility to emotional arousal, with certain individuals exhibiting heightened reactivity and susceptibility to both excitement and rage, while others have lower levels of reactivity and a greater capacity for tolerance.

The development of an individual's personality is influenced by the surrounding environment, including factors such as upbringing and the location in which one is raised. Consequently, a modification in environment has the potential to induce changes in one's personality. However, it is frequently the case that individuals find themselves limited by their own identity, and there is no reason to feel any sense of shame in this regard. However, one's personal identity will ultimately dictate the extent to which they must manage their temper.

Individuals whom you admire and hold in high regard. This pertains not only to one's parents. The topic pertains to individuals' approaches in addressing challenges. It is possible that throughout one's formative years, an individual may have observed a situation in which someone effectively employed anger as a means of response, leading to the inclination to adopt a similar approach. However, upon attempting to undertake the task independently, one will come to the realization that it is not as favorable of a concept as initially perceived.

The emotional state of an individual. This phenomenon significantly influences one's susceptibility to experiencing anger outbursts at various moments. Individuals who are currently experiencing emotional distress are more prone to get agitated by inconsequential matters. On the other hand, a someone who has recently received exceedingly joyous and exhilarating information may exhibit greater magnanimity and acceptance towards circumstances that would otherwise elicit anger.

Experiencing psychological distress. Stress, akin to mood, diverges in that it mostly arises from environmental stimuli rather than individual affective states. The experience of urgency and crisis has the potential to significantly heighten an individual's propensity for anger. Experiencing an overwhelming workload can impair cognitive functioning, leading to heightened emotional reactivity.

Items that are consumed, ingested, or utilized. The physiological components present within an individual's body exert an influence on various aspects of their well-being, including hormonal regulation, mood modulation, stress response, and other related factors. Consequently, these physiological substances also play a role in determining an individual's propensity to experience anger. Naturally, there will be individual variations in this regard.

Alcohol use has been found to potentially heighten an individual's aggression, thereby increasing the likelihood of experiencing anger. However, it has been seen that certain individuals exhibit more timidity when under the influence of alcohol, leading to a higher likelihood of displaying greater levels of tolerance.

Scientific research has demonstrated that nicotine possesses the capacity to mitigate stress levels, hence prompting smokers to employ it as a means of stress reduction. Undoubtedly, this has the detrimental consequence of impairing pulmonary function. Additionally, the reliance on nicotine results in a decreased tolerance for frustration and irritability in the absence of the substance.

Caffeine has the ability to enhance an individual's alertness, resulting in increased responsiveness to both favorable and unfavorable circumstances.

Certain prescribed medications may exhibit adverse effects that can result in increased irritability or feelings of sluggishness.

There exist numerous additional factors that may be incorporated into the aforementioned list; however, the aforementioned points serve as a suitable starting point for reference in the event that one experiences a sense of cognitive disarray once more. Self-awareness is a crucial aspect to consider. One must possess the capability to provide a response to the inquiry: "What is the reason behind my heightened propensity for anger today?" By engaging in this practice, individuals can acquire the knowledge and skills necessary to mitigate the impact of aggravating variables and cultivate strategies that promote emotional tranquility. Further elaboration on this topic will be provided at a later point in time.

What constitutes the concept of anger?

Shock can be described as a deceptive manifestation of animosity against a person or situation that one perceives as having purposely mistreated them. Shock is a frequently seen issue. This resource provides strategies for challenging erroneous beliefs and encourages critical thinking in order to identify effective solutions to problems. Nevertheless, the contemplation of wonder can effectively elucidate the underlying causes of several challenges. The presence of pronounced critical indicators and distinctive physical alterations, which are observed with astonishment, make it exceedingly difficult to promptly and effectively address and mitigate the harm inflicted upon one's physical well-being and overall circumstances. An individual who is feeling amazement may often encounter physical consequences such as an increased heart rate, elevated blood pressure, and heightened levels of adrenaline and vasoconstrictor. Wonder is often seen as a sensation that elicits a component of the fight or flight reaction. The phenomenon of shock undergoes a remarkable transformation, including cognitive, emotional, and physiological aspects, when an individual in a professional setting seizes the discriminating opportunity to swiftly counteract and mitigate the detrimental effects of external pressures. The English term "stomach muscle" originates from the Germanic language, specifically from the term "wonder." The experience of shock is expected to elicit distinct physiological and intellectual consequences. The manifestations of distress in outdoor settings are commonly observed through outward expressions, visible communication, physiological reactions, and very noticeable displays of hostility. The external manifestations will transition from the subtle manipulation of the eyebrows to a complete expression of anger. Despite the fact that the majority of individuals attribute their anger to external factors, mental health professionals argue that anger can also be attributed to a decline in self-regulation and goal differentiation.

The term "stun" could perhaps be considered a brand-specific inclination. Bountiful can be considered proportionate in light of the fact that it aligns with the rest of our sentiments. Regardless, it is imperative that we do not become transformed into hostages, unfortunately. When the moment arrives when your enthusiasm diminishes and begins to intrude upon your personal life, professional endeavors, and interpersonal connections, it becomes a significant issue in our lives. According to a study conducted on the subject of interpersonal relationships, it has been observed that a significant proportion of individuals, specifically 40%, have negative consequences associated with difficulties in managing surprise situations. When individuals accumulate pent-up anger, it can have detrimental effects on both their personal and professional lives. This phenomenon is particularly intriguing when observed within a group of individuals, as it can lead to a sequence of personal and professional setbacks. In order to assist individuals in addressing their burdensome difficulties, organizations such as the British Association of Anger Management exist to provide valuable support.

Alternative Approaches For The Management Of Anger, Anxiety, And Stress

There exist alternative approaches for effectively managing feelings of anger, anxiety, and stress. The following section will examine and analyze the aforementioned topics.

The concept of visualization refers to the process of creating mental images or representations of information, ideas

This approach entails the utilization of one's imagination. One must employ the technique of mental imagery to maintain a state of emotional composure in the face of another individual's anger. Visualize yourself maintaining a composed and tranquil demeanor, even in the face of the other individual's verbal attacks. Imagine maintaining composure in the face of humiliation caused by a fellow coworker.

If an individual has experienced specific events or incidents in their personal history that have elicited feelings of anger, it is suggested that they engage in a mental exercise wherein they imagine and mentally project themselves responding to these situations with a composed and tranquil demeanor. In order to enhance the quality of your visualization, it is imperative to ensure that it is characterized by vividness. This entails incorporating explicit details pertaining to facial expressions and comprehensive descriptions of desired behavioral patterns.

As an illustration, consider the following example:

Suppose that in a previous instance, you experienced frustration due to a colleague who wrongfully appropriated credit for your diligent efforts. You have exhibited a strong emotional reaction, resulting in a reprimand and a tarnish on your otherwise impeccable work history. Nevertheless, you have made a commitment to ensure that such an occurrence does not repeat itself. Thus, one is able to mentally perceive the identical occurrence, albeit with a distinct array of actions. Envision oneself approaching a colleague with purposeful yet composed strides. The individual engages in a conversation with him using a subdued vocal tone, requesting his presence in a secluded location.

Engage in a conversation with the individual in question and assert your legal entitlements as the primary author and owner of the intellectual property. It is important to adopt an assertive communication style while maintaining a respectful demeanor. One potential approach is to seek a compromise that allows for the preservation of ownership over the work. In certain exceptional cases, the individual engaging in plagiarism may exhibit a lack of remorse and persist in asserting authorship of the plagiarized work. In this scenario, it is advisable to solicit evidence from the individual in question to substantiate their claim of being the creator. In the event that circumstances become unmanageable, it is advisable to seek the guidance of a legal professional. It is advisable to delegate the management of legal matters to a qualified attorney. It is preferable for the situation to be handled in that manner rather than engaging in a confrontational argument with him.

It is recommended that one engages in daily visualization practices. The objective of this exercise is to enhance one's ability to maintain a state of composure in the face of anger-inducing circumstances.

Through the process of constant visualization, the absorption of these thoughts by the subconscious mind can lead to a heightened level of automaticity and innate behavior in one's actions.

Understanding and Identifying Anger

The human body serves as a reliable indicator. It presents a series of preliminary indications of anger. The identification of these initial indicators would facilitate the implementation of crucial measures to prevent the escalation of circumstances.

When experiencing anger, individuals may exhibit various physical manifestations.

An increased heart rate

The sensation of a tumbling stomach.

There is an elevation in the individual's core body temperature.

The individual exhibits accelerated respiration.

The phenomenon of experiencing a sudden increase in blood flow to the face.

The act of gnashing one's teeth and clenching one's hands.

Perspiration

The phenomenon of negative thinking

These are preliminary indicators that suggest the presence of potential hazards in the future. The ability to observe and respond appropriately to physical cues plays a crucial role in determining subsequent emotional experiences. Specifically, individuals who are mindful of these signs can either experience feelings of guilt due to losing control and reacting impulsively, or feelings of pride for maintaining composure and effectively managing the situation.

The impact of verbal and physical aggression on children

Can you envision a scenario in which your spouse exhibits a loss of composure and engages in verbal outbursts directed towards you? Consider a hypothetical scenario in which an individual's sustenance, lodging, security, safeguarding, affection, and self-assurance are exclusively reliant upon another person. Consider a scenario in which you find yourself without any alternative sources of support, except for the individuals in question. What is the emotional impact of that on you? Is it frightening? Are you feeling tense? Are you experiencing feelings of anxiety? This sentiment closely resembles the emotional experience children undergo when confronted with parental anger and subsequent loss of self-regulation.

Individuals experience feelings of vulnerability, helplessness, weakness, and disorientation.

It is a common human experience to feel anger towards our children. There is absolutely no reason to feel ashamed about that. However, it is incumbent upon you to maintain emotional regulation and refrain from succumbing to anger, as doing so would mitigate the potential adverse consequences that losing control of your emotions may have on your children.

The act of engaging in verbal abuse, which encompasses name calling, lashing out, and using demeaning language towards one's children, has a profound impact on their mental and emotional well-being. This is due to the fact that children rely on their parents for the development of their self-esteem and sense of self-worth.

It has been documented that children who experience physical violence from their enraged parents exhibit adverse effects in their development. These effects encompass diminished academic achievement, unstable interpersonal relationships, diminished self-worth, increased susceptibility to substance abuse, lack of purpose in life, and an unstable and unfulfilled adulthood.

If children no longer exhibit fear in response to parental anger, it is likely due to their increased familiarity with such expressions and subsequent development of emotional and psychological defenses.

Now, it is imperative to express concern as this implies a decreased inclination to seek approval from authority figures and a heightened preference for peer influence over parental guidance. It is undesirable for parents to have their children's behavior and beliefs more heavily influenced by their peers than by themselves.

It is important to recognize that as one's anger intensifies and is directed towards one's children, they may become desensitized to such behavior. As individuals become increasingly accustomed to a particular situation, their level of consideration towards you and your emotions diminishes. Moreover, the extent to which you can exert a positive influence on your children is diminished. Do you desire that?

Addressing The Physiological Effects Of Anger

The mindfulness instructor emphasized repeatedly that the practice of mindfulness is not centeredaround the mind, but rather focuses on the body. The acquisition of bodily awareness regarding the experience of anger is crucial for discovering solutions and alternative approaches. Although it may initially appear paradoxical to prioritize the body over the mind, it is indeed advantageous to engage with the physical aspects when addressing anger. Awareness can be redirected from the mind, which individuals often find themselves firmly entrenched in, repeatedly experiencing angry thoughts and becoming entangled in them without conscious awareness.

The act of redirecting one's attention to other areas of the body has the potential to disrupt the cycle of anger and facilitate significant therapeutic benefits. Frequently, individuals experience a state of detachment from their physical selves when experiencing anger. We are engaging in contemplation or experiencing an increasing sense of restlessness. A crucial aspect of managing anger involves establishing a connection with the physical manifestations of this emotional state. By doing so, individuals can enhance their ability to regulate anger, recognize its onset, and refrain from acting impulsively in response to it.

Introducing Mindful Awareness to the Physical Body

A significant number of individuals seeking psychotherapy and expressing concerns related to anger management often exhibit challenges in recognizing bodily sensations associated with emotions or engage in behaviors aimed at reducing bodily sensitivity. The impact of bodily stress has been increasingly associated with a wide range of outcomes, ranging from experiencing a challenging day to the development of serious conditions such as cancer and other chronic or life-threatening diagnoses. The physiological mechanisms underlying the stress response and the anger response exhibit considerable overlap. The experience of stress and anger can give rise to bodily manifestations of distress, including but not limited to chronic pain or the development of ulcers. Alternatively, individuals may resort to self-medication through the use of drugs, alcohol, or engaging in addictive behaviors as a means to alleviate these emotional states.

Many aspects of mindfulness practice and anger management techniques appear to contradict common intuition. Individuals experiencing distress may naturally seek to alleviate their suffering by seeking respite from the conscious recognition of pain and adversity. Nevertheless, employing such an approach repeatedly can yield enduring repercussions, making it a short-sighted tactic with far-reaching implications. Buddha unequivocally emphasized, throughout his extensive tenure as a teacher, the imperative of confronting and acquainting ourselves with our suffering in order to effectively address it. It is imperative to raise consciousness regarding the human experience. Throughout the course of history, mindfulness instructors have presented various techniques to direct one's focus towards the physical body. By cultivating this attentiveness, individuals can develop a heightened state of consciousness, which in turn enables them to gain fresh insights, establish new intentions, and engage in transformative actions. Presented here is a brief exercise that employs the breath as a focal point to initiate the process of addressing and ameliorating bodily anger.

Chapter 3: Evaluation of Anger, Aggression, and Domestic Abuse

Experiencing anger is a prevalent phenomenon, as it represents an emotional state or reaction that serves as an indicator of underlying dissatisfaction within our personal circumstances. Anger can be regarded as a prudent reaction to a perceived threat, eliciting our fight or flight responses.

Similar to any other emotion, anger also elicits physiological alterations. The release of adrenaline initiates a physiological response in which it permeates the body, resulting in an elevation of both blood pressure and heart rate. If one has ever expressed or encountered the statement "I am extremely angry to the point where I can sense my blood boiling," it can be argued that they are not far from expressing a valid sentiment.

Developing the ability to manage anger is highly important, as these physiological alterations are also detrimental to one's well-being. A significant proportion of individuals lack the necessary knowledge or skills to effectively manage anger, as it has been reported that approximately one in five Americans experience difficulties in regulating their anger.

Anger is purportedly responsible for a range of issues including road rage, divorce, domestic violence, child abuse, addictions, and workplace aggression. There is a correlation between chronic anger and various physical ailments, such as digestive disorders, sleep disturbances, high blood pressure, chronic headaches, and even myocardial infarctions.

The onset of this phenomenon can be instigated by a relatively insignificant incident, such as a spoken comment or a minor physical accident, such as accidentally hitting one's toe against an object. Emotions frequently exert a dominant influence, overriding any residual rationality that an individual may possess. Currently, individuals have the option to either suppress or manifest their wrath. The suppression of anger can have detrimental effects on both mental and physical well-being, while the expression of rage can be particularly harmful, especially when directed at family, friends, or inanimate objects.

The necessity of anger management classes is readily apparent. The prevalence of rage in contemporary culture is a notable phenomenon, and it presents various implications and outcomes.

Merely peruse news articles. The emotion of anger is pervasive in various contexts. The business in question is of significant magnitude. A film was produced by Hollywood that explores the concept of Anger Management, hence examining its significance. Without a question, the prospect of witnessing the on-screen clash between Adam Sandler and Jack Nicholson would undoubtedly captivate the attention of a wide range of film enthusiasts, regardless of their specific interests. The concept of finding amusement amid rage possesses a distinct appeal. This approach represents a robust method for addressing a significant problem. However, it is worth noting that

Nicholson, in his capacity as an actor, has skillfully portrayed a wide range of rage in various roles. Throughout his career, he has portrayed a number of remarkably dumb and furious characters.

Undoubtedly, there exists a viable economic opportunity pertaining to the emotion of fury. From a social perspective, there exists a simultaneous attraction and aversion towards it. The attractiveness of anger might be likened to the fascination experienced by onlookers at a multiple-vehicle collision, sometimes referred to as "rubbernecking." There exists a discernible area of focus. The experience of anger asserts its influence until it is directly addressed and acknowledged in our personal experiences. Anger poses a substantial obstacle for families. It detrimentally impacts careers, marriages, livelihoods, and overall well-being. The object or subject under consideration exhibits a high degree of opulence or extravagance. Anger exhibits a self-perpetuating and self-propagating nature within social contexts, persisting and spreading from one generation to another.

The Regulation Of Emotional Responses

Emotions exert significant influence over our daily experiences and decision-making processes. The majority of our decision-making processes are influenced by our emotional responses to various experiences or activities. Emotions serve as a means for individuals to express a range of affective states, encompassing both positive and negative sentiments. Interpersonal relationships facilitate comprehension and foster connection among individuals. Nevertheless, interpersonal conflicts might arise as a result of these interactions.

Various fundamental emotions, including anger, happiness, sadness, disgust, surprise, fear, and contempt, are commonly experienced by individuals on different occasions. Emotions can be experienced with varying levels of intensity. These entities have the potential to exist for either a brief or extended duration. The level of concern one exhibits towards a particular event determines their degree of investment in the event.

To initiate the process of emotional management, it is important to have a comprehensive comprehension of the fundamental emotions that underlie one's emotional experiences. Every emotion can be expressed through verbal communication as well as nonverbal cues, such as body language. The communication of emotions to others is frequently facilitated through facial shapes. The process of perceiving and acknowledging the facial expressions that manifest in response to a particular circumstance might facilitate the initiation of strategies aimed at regulating the outward manifestation of one's emotions.

Anger is a prevalent affective state that can be experienced with significant intensity. The experience of this emotion arises when an individual perceives intentional hurt or wrongdoing inflicted against them by another individual. The emotion of anger can present significant challenges as individuals may feel compelled to protect themselves or retaliate against the instigator. The manifestation of anger is perceptible through the physical indicators of tightened lips and lowered eyebrows. The upper and lower eyelids will be elevated, while the corners of the mouth may be inverted. Engaging in facial softening techniques when experiencing anger can serve as an initial step towards regulating this emotional state.

The experience of fear arises when an individual perceives themselves to be in a state of jeopardy. Individuals may have a heightened sense of impending physical or emotional danger, leading to a perceived urge for self-preservation. Protection will be attained by means of the fight or flight response. Fear can be readily identified through facial expressions. The eyebrows will be raised and brought closer, while the lips will exhibit a stretched appearance. The upward retraction of the eyelids and the potential widening of the nostrils may occur. Experiencing dread on a daily basis might lead to the amplification of emotions.

Happiness can be defined as the subjective sense of pleasure or joy. The manifestation of this particular feeling can be observed through the facial expression of a smile. The periorbital muscles will undergo increased tension, resulting in the formation of periorbital wrinkles commonly referred to as crow's feet. It is a positive emotional state that is highly desired by many individuals. An overabundance of happiness may serve as an indicator that an underlying issue or problem is present. Frequently, individuals who are experiencing distress endeavour to conceal their own emotions by outwardly displaying a facade of contentment.

Sadness can be considered as the antithesis of happiness. The experience of emotional discomfort is commonly perceived by individuals. The facial expression is distinguished by the presence of a downward curve of the lips, commonly referred to as a frown. The ocular region may exhibit signs of lacrimation, with the eyebrows displaying elevation in the medial aspects. The eyelids of an individual may also exhibit a lax appearance. Individuals who are afflicted with sadness may perceive themselves as being at a disadvantage, undergoing feelings of grief, disappointment, or bereavement. While experiencing a certain level of melancholy is considered within the range of normal human emotions, an excessive amount of sadness may indicate the presence of a more significant underlying issue.

The perception of emotions is highly subjective, and hence there is no inherent categorization of emotions as right or wrong. There may be instances wherein individuals undergo diverse emotional responses within a given setting. The disparity in emotions might give rise to the occurrence of conflict. It is possible for an individual to see another as being incorrect, however, this perception does not necessarily align with reality. Divergence from the norm does not necessarily imply incorrectness. The manner in which one navigates through the disagreement is of significance. It is imperative to demonstrate respect and endeavour to comprehend the perspective of others. This form of comprehension can facilitate the pursuit of a mutually agreeable solution.

While it is plausible to encounter variations in emotional experiences among individuals, it is possible for some individuals to exhibit heightened emotional intensity, leading to a higher likelihood of engaging in frequent confrontations. For instance, it is possible that you exhibit a propensity for rapid emotional arousal.

Suppose an individual enters a grocery shop with the intention of purchasing milk for their breakfast cereal. While proceeding towards the milk cooler, the observer becomes aware of another individual who is also approaching the same cooler. Given their proximity, it is highly likely that they will arrive at the destination before you. The individual commences the act of waiting with patience for the shopper to conclude their activities. However, it appears that they are exhibiting a prolonged period in reaching their conclusion. As the duration of waiting increases, one's level of impatience correspondingly intensifies. Subsequently, the individual initiates a rhythmic motion of tapping their foot while simultaneously emitting audible exhalations characterised by short, forceful bursts of breath. The individual reverses their direction and offers an expression of remorse. Instead of acknowledging and accepting the situation, you respond with a derogatory remark against their lack of consideration. Upon acquiring the milk, one's heightened emotional state leads to a subsequent deterioration in the overall purchasing experience.

Developing An Understanding Of The Individuals With Whom One Interacts Is Crucial.

One's life is inherently influenced by the others with whom they regularly engage and maintain relationships. Individuals have the potential to intentionally or accidentally provoke emotional reactions from you, and they may possess knowledge of your episodes of wrath. Hence, it is logical to contemplate upon them.

Disorderly interactions give rise to superfluous conflicts and occurrences, substandard outcomes, and ambiguous connections.

All interpersonal exchanges, regardless of the parties involved, consist of three distinct components:

The process of preparing or getting ready for a particular task, event, or situation.

The term "execution" refers to the act of carrying out a planned course of action, The process of post-processing

The division remains consistent regardless of the specific circumstances. In a professional environment, interpersonal exchanges tend to adhere to a more formal and organised framework. Based on my experience, the preparation phase significantly influences approximately 60% of the overall quality of the exchange outcome, while the execution phase accounts for approximately 30%, and post-processing activities contribute approximately 10%.

It is imperative to adequately prepare for every crucial interaction, particularly ones that carry significant consequences. This will aid in maintaining a state of composure and poise during the process of execution. If the preparation is insufficient, a wide range of complications may occur at a later stage.

When considering the process of preparation, it is advantageous to prioritise the following aspects: the content of the interaction, encompassing the subject matter; the goals, which pertain to the underlying purpose; and the people involved, including their respective opinions and the intended audience.

Effective facilitation is essential for promoting successful interactions, while ensuring that all participants possess a clear understanding of their respective roles and responsibilities. It is imperative to establish behavioural rules, whether they be implicit or explicit, for individuals engaging in exchanges, even in one-on-one interactions.

Post-processing facilitates the acquisition of knowledge through the analysis and reflection upon the exchange. Additionally, it serves as a prompt for the participants to recall the events that transpired and underscores the importance of subsequent actions they are required to undertake.

Figure 6: The individuals with whom you engage

Consider the individuals inside the aforementioned analytical framework.

Please proceed to create a circular shape on a sheet of paper.

Position yourself at the centre.

Generate a comprehensive list of individuals with whom you frequently engage and arrange them in proximity to yourself.

After identifying the individuals, proceed to transcribe their names into the designated table provided, subsequently allocating them into the respective quartiles.

The concept of "The Indifferent" refers to a state in which there is a lack of engagement or emotional involvement. The individual in question can be characterised as a peripheral figure, akin to an auxiliary cast member in a theatrical production.

The Neutral: The majority of contacts consist of brief exchanges characterised by service-oriented transactions and encounters, lacking any substantial relational connections.

The happy: Interactions engender a sense of upliftment, leading to the formation of relationships and the experience of happy feelings.

The Detrimental Aspect: The perplexing and emotionally exhausting exchanges and intricate connections give rise to adverse affective states.

The act of labelling and discerning is employed to gain comprehension and enhance interactions and relationships.

This will additionally assist us in predicting stimuli that elicit rage.

These aforementioned methods are effective in the management and regulation of sudden and intense episodes of rage. However, those who experience persistent anger problems should undertake additional measures beyond the aforementioned three steps. Listed below are several other strategic approaches to acquiring control and managing rage effectively.

Regular physical exercise is an essential component of maintaining a healthy lifestyle. Regular physical exercise is an effective method for acquiring anger management skills. Engaging in exercise triggers the release of neurotransmitters such as dopamine and serotonin within the body, resulting in notable enhancements in one's mental state and reduced vulnerability to anger. Moreover, engaging in physical activity can serve as an effective method for alleviating stress. Consequently, if your anger is triggered by stress, incorporating exercise into your routine can be an advantageous approach for effectively managing and regulating your anger.

The Utilisation of Relaxation Techniques for Stress Reduction An other method for acquiring skills in anger management is the utilisation of relaxation techniques. Allocate a period of alone to engage in introspection and employ this opportunity to engage in the practise of meditation and achieve a state of relaxation. Engaging in these activities can enhance one's ability to cope with stress and frustration, thereby reducing the likelihood of experiencing anger.

Articulate Your Feelings: Engage in a conversation regarding your emotions with a trusted confidant, such as a close friend or family member. For individuals who possess introverted or reserved tendencies and prefer not to engage in emotional discussions with others, it may be advisable to initiate the practise of maintaining an angry notebook. One potential strategy for managing anger is the utilisation of an anger journal, wherein individuals can document their emotions and engage in uninhibited self-expression. Engaging in this practise facilitates the avoidance of emotional suppression as well as the prevention of unhealthy emotional expression.

The concept of not holding grudges entails the necessity of cultivating the ability to release one's feelings of anger and resentment. It is imperative to refrain from allowing notions of global injustice or personal opposition to exert influence over one's cognitive processes. Eliminate thoughts that incite anger and cultivate a state of mental clarity and purity.

Developing Assertiveness Skills: The concept of assertiveness is acquiring the ability to effectively pursue one's desires while simultaneously taking into account the emotions and sentiments of others.

The absence of proficiency in employing these strategies to acquire anger management skills independently serves as an indication that it is opportune for individuals to pursue expert assistance in addressing their issue.

In this discourse, we shall endeavour to identify potential solutions to the prevailing issue at hand.

The second step involves generating a range of prospective solutions, encompassing various options, reactions, or courses of action that can be pursued in order to address the situation at hand. The objective is to construct a variety of prospective solutions, akin to a menu of choices. One facet of this strategy involves adopting a divergent mindset towards problems and discerning potential courses of action that deviate from conventional considerations. Initially, individuals may feel themselves gravitating towards an excessively radical resolution. One possible course of action could involve contacting the authorities to inform them about the situation and expressing the intention to pursue a restraining order against one's former spouse in the event of their communication. The prevalence of such radical prospective solutions is widespread and within the bounds of normalcy. During episodes of anger, individuals frequently experience cognitive processes characterised by limited and skewed thinking patterns. However, when initiating the process of seeing several alternative options, it becomes increasingly feasible to discern more efficacious resolutions. If the proposed remedies appear to exacerbate the existing problem, it is advisable to persist in generating alternative possibilities.

Through consistent effort, one will ultimately generate multiple viable choices, leading to a gradual facilitation of the entire process with continued use. In the interim, please proceed with generating a spectrum of possibilities, encompassing those that are expected to be entirely ineffectual to those that are viable for implementation. The number of potential solutions that can be identified is contingent upon the nature of the problem, the level of creativity exhibited, and the extent of practise undertaken. It is advisable to generate a minimum of five prospective solutions, with the possibility of exploring additional alternatives for enhanced outcomes.

This analysis aims to identify the probable short-term outcomes.

Short-term consequences refer to the instant responses that individuals are anticipated to receive from others. It is important to exercise caution, as exclusively prioritising immediate outcomes may lead to errors in judgement. For instance, in the event of experiencing anger, one may engage in yelling at their son as a response to his altercation with his sister, potentially resulting in the son's quick acquiescence. In the context of a prolonged duration, it is likely that engaging in verbal aggression against one's son would result in the development of emotional detachment within the parent-child connection, while also serving as a negative example of conduct for the child. Despite the potential lack of perfect clarity regarding the anticipated short-term outcome, it is generally feasible to formulate an informed speculation regarding the consequences that may ensue upon pursuing a specific course of action. The objective is to determine the conclusion that is most probable.

This analysis aims to identify the probable long-term outcomes.

Long-term outcomes refer to the results that manifest gradually and persist over extended periods, spanning from hours to days, months, and even years. For instance, engaging in physical violence or inflicting harm on others or their belongings with the intention of imparting a lesson may provide immediate gratification. However, over an extended period, engaging in such behaviour can lead to legal issues that are time-consuming, disruptive, and financially burdensome. In situations when a probable long-term result is not readily apparent, it is advisable to formulate an informed conjecture regarding the outcome that is most probable.

Identify the optimal solution and implement it effectively.

When evaluating the probable short- and long-term consequences of any prospective resolution, it is advisable not to dismiss any solution until a comprehensive assessment of all available alternatives has been conducted. The selection procedure should commence by rejecting prospective solutions that are improbable to yield favourable outcomes. It is important to have a realistic approach when striving to identify the optimal answer. It is vital to contemplate the requisite talents necessary to undertake a particular path of action. Otherwise, individuals may inadvertently commit the frequent error of selecting a solution that exceeds their proficiency in execution, despite the fact that said solution is very probable to yield the most favourable result.

Acknowledging The Presence Of An Anger-Related Condition

Once individuals acknowledge that anger only leads to internal emotional distress, they become prepared to progress by engaging in a more explicitly defined course of good activity.

Catherine Pulsifer is a notable individual.

It is probable that one has encountered instances in which an individual experiences anger, responds in an explosive manner, and thereafter offers an apology accompanied by the common justification of being unaware of their actions.

Repeatedly hearing the same excuse can be fatiguing, particularly when one is aware that such behaviour is likely to recur in the near future. At times, individuals find themselves in the position of providing excuses, a repetitive occurrence that can be exasperating, leading to a tendency to overlook or disregard such excuses.

However, it should be noted that the issue has not been completely eradicated or resolved. The act of concealing ourselves is currently being undertaken, and it is imperative that this behaviour be discontinued.

A common tendency among individuals is to engage in avoidance strategies when confronted with personal challenges, whether they are of a physical, mental, or emotional kind, by adopting a pretence of nonexistence. This phenomenon is commonly referred to as avoidance coping.

This particular coping mechanism frequently results in negative consequences. It significantly disrupts all aspects of one's life, including interpersonal connections and psychological well-being. Uncontrolled anger has the potential to lead to the deterioration of interpersonal relationships if it is not well managed.

At times, individuals may engage in self-deception regarding the presence of anger issues. However, if one consistently experiences episodes of intense anger, characterised by frequent outbursts, verbal aggression towards others, and a persistent belief that others fail to comprehend one's perspective, it becomes necessary to acknowledge the existence of anger difficulties.

The initial stage in the process of healing is the act of acceptance. This opens a pathway for more therapeutic interventions. There exists a saying that posits the notion that while it is possible to guide a horse to a body of water, it remains beyond one's capacity to compel the horse to partake in drinking from it. It might be asserted that until an individual demonstrates a willingness to undergo transformation, no external entity have the capacity to compel such change.

Examining the impact of one's angry outbursts on the individuals affected is a crucial undertaking. Does it elicit feelings of grief, sorrow, and disappointment? If such is the case, I am of the opinion that it is now opportune to initiate a transformation.

Numerous circumstances prompted me to undergo a transformation, although the most notable occurrence was during my ninth-grade year. During a verbal disagreement with a fellow student of higher academic standing, I regrettably succumbed to a fit of intense fury, resulting in physical contact in the form of striking the individual's facial region. To this day, my memory fails to recollect the precise catalyst for my intense anger that precipitated the regrettable action. However, the profound emotional distress that ensued from that action remains indelibly etched in my consciousness.

Anger is a spontaneous emotional response that disregards rational deliberation. The prompt requests a response, and the only means by which the intensity of that rage can be reduced is through the exercise of self-regulation. The therapeutic interventions for individuals with explosive anger

There are several therapeutic options that can be employed to address the issue of intense and uncontrollable rage. In situations where one observes that the outbursts exhibit antisocial tendencies and pose potential risks to oneself and others, the implementation of medication may become necessary. Typically, short-term interventions are designed to promptly address the issue at hand and mitigate its impact, allowing for the subsequent introduction of alternative approaches. The efficacy of the drug may diminish gradually over a period of time.

Nevertheless, the majority of individuals do not require immediate medicine. A range of interventions exists with the aim of instructing individuals with anger difficulties on the skills necessary for anger management and the ability to identify their anger. One illustrative instance involves the utilisation of cognitive behavioural therapy (CBT) as a means to impart knowledge to an individual regarding the identification of ideas that may provoke anger. Individuals have the capacity to substitute these thoughts with more composed and constructive ones, which can aid in the cessation of rage and the subsequent escalation of negative consequences associated with their outbursts.

Biofeedback can be utilised in combination with cognitive-behavioral therapy (CBT) as well as alone as a standalone intervention. In this approach, the individual will be provided with a heart rate monitor. Individuals can discern their impending anger by perceiving an elevation in their heart rate. Individuals will have this realisation and ideally possess the ability to promptly halt its progression. This intervention is beneficial for those who may lack awareness or fail to identify the signs of anger they are experiencing, and who may want direction and assistance in managing their anger.

The aforementioned techniques represent a limited selection of strategies that can be employed to effectively manage one's anger. Acquiring the skill of cultivating a positive mindset, familiarising oneself with the indicators and manifestations of escalating aggression, and acquiring effective anger management techniques might contribute to mitigating the challenges associated with such circumstances.

Factors contributing to anger control difficulties.

There exist numerous factors that can elicit feelings of wrath. The variation of these aspects is frequently observed among individuals. Several prevalent factors contributing to violence include:

the presence of threats and unjust treatment, instances of public humiliation, personal challenges such as financial difficulties or work-related stress, past traumatic experiences, and the experience of losing a family member or friend.

Regardless of the underlying factors contributing to one's anger, it is crucial to recognise the capacity to regulate and manage this emotional state in order to prevent any adverse consequences for oneself and others.

Anger can be manifested through either passive or outward means, and it may appear that those in one's vicinity serve as the catalyst for such negative emotional responses. Nevertheless, the act of projecting can be understood as the outcome of one's subjective assessment of a given scenario inside their cognitive framework. The subsequent cognitive processes play a crucial role in determining one's ability to regulate anger and choose appropriate responses.

Several notable negative patterns that have the potential to elicit rage issues encompass, although not only, the subsequent factors.

The statement made is a generalisation.

The predominant catalyst for the experience of rage often stems from a tendency to interpret situations in an unfavourable manner, mostly through the process of overgeneralization. One potential cognitive distortion involves the tendency to generalise instances of feeling disrespected, leading to the belief that everyone holds a negative perception of oneself based on a single disrespectful event. It is important to bear in mind that making broad generalisations often leads to conclusions that are significantly divergent from reality. Instead than engaging in a broad analysis, it is recommended to approach each circumstance individually, without making sweeping generalisations. This approach has been found to effectively mitigate feelings of rage.

I currently hold a fixed perspective on the external environment.

In many instances, individuals may exhibit a reluctance to deviate from their own subjective viewpoints and preconceived notions on the nature of phenomena and their preferred conceptual frameworks. When delivering a project presentation inside a professional setting, it is common to encounter a minority of individuals who may express disagreement with your views and attempt to pose challenges. However, it is possible to hold a differing viewpoint and subsequently experience a transformation of that perspective into a state of wrath. Nevertheless, rather than perceiving your perspectives as a personal affront to your intellectual capabilities, it is imperative to adopt a composed demeanour and articulate the reasons why those other approaches may not be suitable for your project or how your notion surpasses them in superiority. Engaging in the practise of self-regulation and achieving a state of calmness might facilitate cognitive clarity, without necessarily impeding one's ability to exercise sound judgement and without provoking feelings of rage.

Theoretical framework refers to the conceptual structure that guides the development and organisation of a research study. It provides a foundation for understanding the

The literature research conducted has revealed the intricate nature of the anger phenomena as it manifests within modern civilizations. To comprehensively analyse the development of this phenomenon as a societal problem or mental health disease, we suggest adopting a theoretical framework that combines constructivist and interactionist perspectives, while also incorporating elements inspired by the works of Michel Foucault.

2.1. The Constructivist Paradigm in the Study of Social Problems

According to Loriol (2012), the constructivist approach postulates that the reality we perceive and the information we possess are, to some extent, influenced by our own activities. In essence, it can be argued that the entirety of reality is influenced, to some extent, by a subjective interpretation that is shaped by both individual perspectives and shared understandings within a particular societal context. Although certain items or social conditions may appear to exist independently and objectively in everyday life, our comprehension, our connection, and our response to them exhibit variations. The human tendency to assign significance to our surroundings is a persistent endeavour, as it is through this process that we establish connections with both the divine and our fellow beings. Despite its ubiquity, every individual ascribes their own personal meanings to the world, which serves as the foundation for their understanding and perception of it. The various interpretations of these meanings engage in mutual influence, occasionally resulting in contradictions, yet ultimately contributing to the formation of a shared understanding within a specific context. Hence, it might be argued that the existence of a singular, objective reality is absent, giving way to a reality that is constructed upon the perceptions and interpretations of individuals and their shared subjectivities.

From a young age, each human undergoes a process of socialisation, through which they develop interpretive frameworks for understanding the world surrounding them. The process of socialisation is an ongoing and continual phenomenon, as new interpretative models or information are introduced to existing established models, potentially leading to their modification. The translation of subjective processes that form a particular reality occurs through the utilisation of several objectification approaches. Loriol (2012) cites Pierre Bourdieu's perspective on construction as a dialectical process including the externalisation of interiority (habitus as systems of disposition) and the internalisation of the exterior (social structures) (p. 25). Berger and Luckmann (1986) provide further support for this theory. Based on these findings, it can be argued that the interaction between the individual and the social environment in which they are situated is characterised by a dialectical interplay. Put simply, individuals will play a role in shaping the social environment by expressing their personal thoughts and experiences in relation to existing realities. This externalisation process involves objectifying their subjective consciousness. Conversely, individuals will also internalise external influences and incorporate them into their own consciousness through similar processes. The act of objectification serves to depersonalise and devalue the many aspects of the surrounding universe. He assumes the dual role of both the creator and recipient of his social environment. Within the realm of objectification, various devices can be identified, including the system of classification (sometimes referred to as typification as proposed by Berger and Luckmann), statistical data, media and political statements, material devices, language, gestures, institutions, and so forth. Language plays a crucial role in the process of objectifying various aspects of reality. The process of socialisation is typically derived from it, as it imparts meaning to things and social experiences, and primarily facilitates the accessibility of our subjectivities to the wider society. Language has a significant role in the formation of categories or typifications, enabling individuals to distinguish and comprehend various aspects within the social realm. These categories are employed to comprehend the conditions encountered and depend on them to navigate our everyday social interactions. The utilisation of these objectification mechanisms will generate what Berger and Luckmann (1986) refer to as the "social stock of knowledge," which is created through intersubjectiveinteractions and disseminated across the social sphere. Each individual assimilates knowledge in a manner that is unique to their personal circumstances and available resources.

The existence of a collective global experience and the resultant shared understanding necessitate the establishment of institutional integration, as posited by Berger and Luckmann (1986). The institutional order encompasses a body of knowledge that establishes norms governing the acceptable behaviours to be observed. Furthermore, the process of institutionalisation is characterised by the establishment of a categorization system, which serves to determine the permissible behaviours and assign specific roles to individuals based on these categories (Berger and Luckmann, 1986). This suggests the presence of a mechanism for regulating human conduct, as it establishes prescribed behavioural norms that therefore urge individuals to act in manners that align with the objectives of the respective institution. The process of institutionalisation can take on either an informal or formal nature. In the informal sense, it involves the acceptance and shared adherence to rules within a social group, even if these rules are not explicitly documented. In the formal sense, institutionalisation entails the translation of rules into a theoretical framework, thereby providing legitimacy to the actions undertaken (Berger and Luckmann, 1986). According to Berger and Luckmann (1986, p.105), all institutionalised behaviour involves the assumption of specific roles. Consequently, each individual assumes a function that allows them to contribute to the development of the social world. Simultaneously, by internalising this social world, individuals assign significance to their surroundings. Henceforth, it can be observed that each societal job is linked to a distinct segment of the collective body of knowledge, leading to the emergence of specialised knowledge within various groups of persons. According to Berger and Luckmann (1986), specialists possess information pertaining to specific realities, which subsequently informs their guidance of related behaviours within their respective domains of expertise.

If we consider knowledge to be a collection of universally accepted truths about the nature of reality, any departure from the established system is seen as a departure from reality. According to Berger and Luckmann (1986, p. 93), In order to maintain the integrity of the existing reality, it is imperative to develop a conceptual framework to comprehend and analyse these deviations. Put differently, the emergence of these novel aberrant phenomena necessitates the construction of a distinct corpus of knowledge that is tailored to comprehending and interpreting them. When should one seek assistance?

Parents often express concern and seek guidance regarding their young child's displays of anger and aggression. It is advisable to seek guidance from a medical professional if your toddler exhibits numerous and intense episodes of anger throughout the day, despite your attempts to address and regulate their behaviour. Additionally, if your toddler's tantrums persist for prolonged durations and you hold concerns regarding the potential for self-inflicted harm or harm to others during these episodes, speaking with a healthcare provider is recommended.

Aggressive behaviour is commonly observed during the initial phases of childhood development. Nevertheless, if a child's display of antagonism is impeding their capacity to effectively interact, explore, and acquire knowledge.In situations where a parent restricts their child's interactions with peers and participation in social activities due to the child's aggressive conduct, seeking guidance from a child development expert would be a more advisable course of action.

In the event that an infant exhibits signs of distress and there is a suspicion of illness or discomfort, it is imperative to promptly seek medical assistance. Nevertheless, if the infant is in good health, easily comforted, and displays signs of well-being during periods of intense crying. It is advisable to exercise caution in one's response to the outbursts exhibited by individuals. In the event that an infant exhibits a challenging temperament, it is of utmost importance to maintain a state of calmness or assign caregiving responsibilities to others as necessary. Infants possess the ability to perceive heightened levels of tension or impatience in individuals, prompting them to potentially exhibit an amplified vocal response through increased crying.

There is a higher probability of a toddler experiencing a state of calmness when the individuals in their immediate environment exhibit positive emotions. Several studies have suggested that infants with challenging temperaments are more prone to positively respond to calm and soothing parenting techniques compared to infants with more stable temperaments.

There is no need for concern regarding the act of yielding to an infant's cries or tantrums, as it is advisable to promptly attend to their needs. Modifying the attitude of one's child may prove to be a challenging endeavour, necessitating the exploration of novel strategies to effectively pacify their emotional state. Nevertheless, it is advisable to consult with your child's healthcare provider in the event that your infant consistently exhibits distress or experiences symptoms of colic, in order to eliminate the possibility of an underlying medical ailment.Certain patterns necessitate additional scrutiny when they frequently manifest and endure over a prolonged period. For illustrative purposes, let us examine the outcomes that arise when a child:

Demonstrates a seemingly audacious or intrepid disposition, characterised by a daring and adventurous approach to existence. This approach frequently leads to the breakage of items or the engagement in intrusive actions, such as encroaching upon the personal space of others.

The individual exhibits a strong desire for sensory experiences characterised by high levels of intensity. Children who require a significant amount of physical contact in order to maintain their attention may exhibit adverse reactions to sensory feedback, such as engaging in hitting, shoving, pushing, and similar behaviours.

Exhibits unprovoked physical aggression; displays sudden and inexplicable violent behaviour.

Demonstrates a strong inclination towards themes of violence.In the context of imaginative play.

After experiencing a traumatic event or undergoing a significant life change, the individual exhibits aggressive behaviour.

The occurrence of anger in toddlers is considered within the realm of normal behaviour and does not warrant concern if it is of short duration, even if it manifests on a regular basis. It is advisable to seek guidance from a medical professional in the event that your child's tantrums escalate in severity, persist for extended durations, or manifest unexpectedly. It is advisable to consult a paediatrician in cases where tantrums exhibit excessive physicality or pose a risk to individuals, including the toddler. The physician may advise parents to monitor and document their child's episodes of anger or tantrums in order to ascertain the root cause. Additionally, individuals have the opportunity to investigate diverse approaches for mitigating their agitation.

In the event that a child's tantrums exhibit an increased frequency or severity beyond the norm, it is possible for a medical practitioner to provide a referral to a child development specialist or a mental health professional in order to obtain appropriate assistance.

Tantrums are a common occurrence among toddlers who are experiencing anger. When faced with a tantrum exhibited by a toddler, it is advisable to employ effective parenting strategies tailored to their specific needs and developmental stage. Establishing a consistent daily schedule and supporting your child in effectively communicating their emotions can be effective strategies for preventing or minimising episodes of tantrums. However, it will not be feasible to prevent all of them.

Tantrums are a prevalent aspect of the developmental trajectory of toddlers. Nevertheless, seeking expert guidance and implementing timely interventions can potentially assist in enhancing your child's ability to manage frustration more efficiently over an extended period of time. Over time, this will provide assistance to your child in educational environments, domestic settings, and various other contexts.

The Sociocultural Factors Contributing To The Experience Of Anger.

The proliferation of the internet and social media platforms has led to an escalation in the standards we establish for our personal and familial spheres, which can be deemed as unattainable. Frequently, our perception of the ideal family structure is influenced by the portrayals we encounter on social media platforms. The frustration arises when our children or partners do not conform to the idealised image we have in mind.

Nevertheless, it is important to acknowledge that the depiction of reality in social media platforms is not always subject to the same level of filtration. In order to liberate oneself from impractical expectations, it is imperative to make the conscious decision to disengage from the notion of an idealised social media family construct. Amongst ourselves, it is important to acknowledge that the concept of a flawless family is non-existent.

In the present scenario, the source of concern may not necessarily be social media platforms, but rather the neighbouring household. The individuals in question appear to lead an idealised existence, characterised by a child who exhibits fewer instances of disruptive behaviour compared to one's own offspring, as well as a partner who displays a greater degree of empathy and consideration. However, it is important to acknowledge that there is significant variation among families, and no two families can be considered identical. Engaging in a comparison between oneself or one's family and a seemingly flawless counterpart entails disregarding one's own distinctiveness and establishing unrealistic expectations, which can lead to disappointment when one's child deviates from the idealised image.

Similar to individuals of the human species, it is inevitable that your child will commit errors. It is likely that the child will cause damage or deterioration to the recently acquired garments. It is observed that young children often fail to complete their dinner within a timeframe that allows parents to promptly attend to dishwashing duties on a daily basis. Developing the ability to recognise the inherent humanity in one's child can contribute to cultivating a sense of calmness and patience when confronted with their imperfect behaviours. Opt for perceiving your family as a dynamic entity that is constantly evolving, rather than an idealised and flawless unit. By adopting this approach, individuals can effectively address the inevitable occurrence of errors in a compassionate and light-hearted manner.

One recommended course of action

Engage in introspection and contemplation. What are some impractical expectations that you hold for your offspring? It is important to consider that one's offspring is in a state of childhood. It is advisable to refrain from evaluating one's child solely from an adult perspective.

An alternative approach to managing unrealistic expectations involves the practise of expressing gratitude. The following procedure outlines the steps: Given the prevailing societal inclination towards prioritising perfection over progress, individuals frequently encounter a recurring cycle of self-inflicted distress, wherein their attention is disproportionately fixated on their shortcomings rather than acknowledging their accomplishments. Individuals often tend to adopt a predisposition towards unhappiness regarding their unfulfilled desires, rather than cultivating a sense of gratitude for their existing possessions and circumstances.

In truth, gratitude is not solely a behavioural manifestation, but rather a cognitive and affective state. Gratitude is a deliberate choice to maintain a state of contentment regarding the aspects of life that unfold as intended, rather than fixating on the minor intricacies that deviate from our initial expectations.

In what manner does expressing gratitude contribute to managing feelings of anger?

If one's experience of anger arises from holding unrealistic expectations, cultivating gratitude can provide the capacity to direct attention towards positive attributes, while also allowing for the recognition of areas in need of improvement. Ultimately, it can be regarded as an expression of self-affection and self-elegance. Expressing gratitude towards others can contribute to a reduction in one's tendency to be overly critical of their actions. This perspective allows for a comprehensive understanding of an individual's identity and the level of satisfaction derived from their presence in one's life. In this particular scenario, the individual in question could potentially be identified as one's offspring. The experience of gratitude engenders a profound sense of joy within an individual, rendering it more effortless to assuage the intense flames of anger as they arise.

Recognising and acknowledging one's feelings of anger.

The constructive utilisation of anger commences with the constructive manifestation of anger. There are four techniques that can be employed, as deemed appropriate, to facilitate the expression of anger in a manner that is both constructive and beneficial. The aforementioned strategies encompass the act of recognising one's anger, determining the root cause of said anger, contemplating the viewpoint of the other individual involved, and subsequently implementing appropriate measures.

Recognising one's anger is crucial for effectively harnessing and channelling it towards constructive outcomes. Individuals frequently categorise their experience of anger using alternative terms. However, by refraining from doing so, the potential advantages of harnessing anger in a constructive manner are forfeited.

Could you please provide an answer to my query?

To what extent are you proficient in recognising and acknowledging your experience of anger?

The available choices are:

The performance was commendable.

The user's response is acceptable.

The performance is unsatisfactory.

The response provided by the user is insufficient to generate an academic rewrite. Please provide a more

Option 1: It is likely that you are already aware of the significance of acknowledging and acknowledging one's anger. Opting to employ anger in a constructive manner can enable individuals to effectively utilise its potential in order to yield favourable results for themselves, their peers, and ultimately, their employer.

Option 2: The ability to acknowledge one's anger can facilitate the redirection of this emotion towards constructive objectives. The potential reluctance to acknowledge one's anger may stem from societal norms that discourage the expression of this emotion due to its perceived lack of professionalism. Acknowledging and articulating one's anger can be employed as a means to foster advantageous results within the professional setting. If left unmanaged, anger can significantly impact productivity within the workplace.

Option 3: It is possible that individuals may choose to suppress or misidentify their anger by attributing it to alternative emotions such as distress, fear, guilt, or feelings of inadequacy. It is possible that you have acquired the knowledge that the expression of anger is discouraged. Recognising and acknowledging one's anger empowers individuals to effectively manage and channel their anger in a constructive manner, thereby avoiding the detrimental consequences of prolonged anger, heightened tension, and festering resentment.

Both Amy and Pascal occupy managerial positions and frequently collaborate on project assignments. Amy strongly dislikes collaborating with Pascal due to her perceived lack of competence in his presence.

In the ensuing dialogue, Amy and her colleague, Jessica, engage in a conversation regarding the emotional impact of Pascal on Amy.

Jessica expressed her perplexity regarding the ability to tolerate Pascal's lack of respect. I would experience significant displeasure if he were to treat me in a manner similar to how he treats you.

Amy's statement is accurate. Jessica, I am experiencing feelings of anger. Throughout the duration, I have consistently suppressed my anger by attributing it to my personal inadequacy.

Jessica reassured Amy that her perceived incompetence was not the cause of the situation. Suppressing one's anger is detrimental to one's well-being. It is imperative for individuals to assume accountability for their emotional responses, particularly anger, and effectively address the conflict at hand with Pascal.

Amy concurs with your statement. I believe that I am entitled to receive respect, however, Pascal has not demonstrated any such respect towards me. Moreover, it is imperative to adopt a responsible approach by effectively managing and processing my feelings of anger, which will ultimately enhance my level of productivity.

With the assistance of Jessica, Amy has successfully ceased misattributing her anger as a manifestation of incompetence. The individual has come to the realisation that it is incumbent upon her to assume accountability for her anger. Recognising and acknowledging one's anger can facilitate a deeper comprehension of its underlying causes, while assuming personal responsibility for this emotional state can empower individuals to effectively manage and regulate their anger.

When expressing anger in a professional setting, it is beneficial to adhere to certain guidelines in order to effectively channel this emotion. It is important to maintain a respectful demeanour, directing attention towards the source of anger rather than individuals involved, and harnessing the energy provided by anger to one's advantage.

Please choose each guideline for effectively channelling anger towards personal growth and learning.

The Fundamentals of an Agitated Brain

The brain in a state of anger exhibits numerous characteristics that gradually evolve into ingrained habits, ultimately manifesting as persistent patterns of behaviour that prove challenging to modify or cease. Every individual brain that experiences anger possesses a sophisticated cognitive system characterised by a unique linguistic framework. However, the manifestation of this anger-related cognitive process does not present any concerns until certain specific factors are encountered, which may include, but are not limited to, the following:

Individuals may experience a heightened propensity for anger, whether it is a conscious or subconscious response.

Individuals may experience heightened agitation and excessive excitement in response to anger.

The presence of anger can impede one's ability to maintain productivity due to its negative impact on cognitive functioning and the subsequent challenge of regaining focus.

Individuals often experience a sense of remorse following impulsive behaviours that are triggered by anger.

Individuals may experience challenges in maintaining focus on a given task or comprehending information when experiencing feelings of anger.

Resentment may arise as a result of internalising anger rather than expressing it outwardly.

One experiences a sense of loss of control when overwhelmed by intense anger.

Frequent experiences of anger can significantly influence one's overall perspective, leading to the development of a belief that a majority, if not all, individuals are adversaries.

Ultimately, if one fails to exercise proper control over their anger, it has the potential to permeate and define their very being. Although it may not have occurred at present, there is a possibility that with the passage of time, an individual's brain, when experiencing anger, could potentially develop such dominance that their irrational outbursts of anger or sustained passive-aggressive behaviour may appear justified and entirely ordinary.

The Importance of Sustaining a Support Network

The management of anger is a complex undertaking that can have a significant emotional toll and may not always be feasible to accomplish independently. Hence, the establishment of a support system is potentially the pivotal element in facilitating one's progress through the aforementioned process.

Communicate one's intentions to another individual. It is imperative for individuals facing challenges to confide in a trusted individual, such as a parent, friend, or spouse, who possesses knowledge regarding their predicament and their ongoing efforts to resolve it. Receiving assistance from a supportive individual who can provide motivation following setbacks, as well as offer objective evaluations of one's progress, can prove highly beneficial.

Enhancing communication can serve as a potential remedy for anger, as the absence of a support system may contribute to its emergence. Perhaps the persistent experience of anger towards one's coworkers may be attributed to a lack of attentiveness towards their perspectives and a failure to comprehend their viewpoints. The potential cause of conflict between spouses may arise from a situation where both individuals aspire to enhance their mutual happiness, yet exhibit an unwillingness to compromise on their respective beliefs. Engaging in open-minded conversations and actively seeking to comprehend others' perspectives can potentially alleviate the underlying factors contributing to one's feelings of frustration. Similar to oneself, individuals possess their own perspectives, and divergences of opinion need not necessarily imply the fallacy of one party.

Devote a portion of your time to individuals whom you hold affection for – A prevailing belief among psychologists is that a significant cause of contemporary frustration and stress stems from the absence of effective interpersonal communication. Engaging in a ten-hour workday followed by arriving home fatigued significantly restricts the amount of quality time available for interpersonal connection with one's romantic partner. It is imperative to acknowledge the importance of allocating time for loved ones and subsequently adhere to the commitments made. Allocate one day per week devoid of specific work objectives, allowing oneself to embrace spontaneity and adapt to the circumstances. Engage in social activities with individuals who hold significant personal value, partake in a rejuvenating stroll, or alternatively, remain indoors to engage in meaningful conversation and establish interpersonal connections. The experience of love, both in giving and receiving, has the potential to serve as a powerful source of positive energy capable of mitigating negative emotions such as anger, stress, frustration, and hostility.

Documenting Your Advancement and Maintaining Perseverance

Managing anger can pose significant challenges as individuals may experience frustration when their chosen strategies fail to yield desired results. Following a period of successfully managing one's anger for a span of two days, experiencing an episode of anger on the third day may evoke a sense of stagnation and regression in one's efforts, reminiscent of the initial stage of addressing the issue.

To mitigate the experience of failure, various strategies can be employed to foster a positive mindset.

Assuming Accountability For One's Anger

As previously mentioned, the individual who bears sole responsibility for one's emotional state is oneself. The experience of irritation, frustration, or anger is not solely determined by the behaviour of others, but rather by one's own response to such behaviour. By assuming accountability for one's reactions, it becomes feasible to effectively regulate one's anger.

When encountering a distressing situation, it is crucial to reflect upon the underlying reasons for one's emotional response. Subsequently, it is imperative to extrapolate these reasons to comprehend the potential motivations behind the individual's behaviour or reaction that elicits distress. Compassion and empathy are regarded as highly valuable tools in one's repertoire. Gaining insight into the motivations behind an individual's dishonesty or unkind behaviour can facilitate the process of forgiveness and subsequent emotional progression. Choosing to let go of past grievances is a more favourable decision, rather than allowing another individual's actions to incite anger and detrimentally impact one's life.

It is imperative to bear in mind that comprehending anger does not entail its utilisation as a justification. One may possess an understanding of the underlying motivations behind an individual's act of deception, yet this comprehension does not imply a disregard or dismissal of the falsehood itself. One can choose to react to such a situation not with anger, but with a mindset of comprehension. Once more, this does not imply that you are neglecting or disregarding the falsehood.

In the final analysis, it is imperative to introspect and pose the fundamental query: "Does the value of my anger outweigh the detrimental consequences it will inflict upon my personal existence, physical well-being, and overall welfare?" The response consistently and unequivocally remains negative. The expression of anger is not justified in any circumstance.

Assuming accountability for one's own anger entails refraining from assuming accountability for the anger exhibited by others. The attribution of fault for anger lies neither with the individual experiencing anger nor with the individual who may be the target of that anger. When confronted with a situation where an individual, such as a friend, coworker, or spouse, responds with anger, it is crucial to acknowledge that their reaction is a result of conditioning. The cognitive processes of their brains have not yet acquired the ability to generate distinct responses.

If individuals in your social circle exhibit similar challenges with anger management as you do, it may be worth contemplating the possibility of forming a collaborative alliance to collectively address and overcome the ingrained behavioural patterns that are detrimentally impacting your respective lives, overall health, and general welfare.

Having a companion who can provide emotional support during times of emotional distress can be beneficial. An individual who possesses the ability to serve as a reminder when one is exhibiting excessive emotional responses. An individual capable of providing gentle encouragement for engaging in meditation practises. Similarly, the reciprocal action can be performed towards them.

www.ingramcontent.com/pod-product-compliance
Lightning Source LLC
Chambersburg PA
CBHW052142110526
44591CB00012B/1830